D1426637

Council

3013021119728 9

Strictly
Ballroom

Strictly Ballroom

Tales from the Dancefloor

DIANA MELLY

Published in 2015 by
Short Books, Unit 316, ScreenWorks,
22 Highbury Grove,
London N5 2ER

10 9 8 7 6 5 4 3 2 1

Copyright © Diana Melly 2015

Diana Melly has asserted her right under the Copyright,
Designs and Patents Act 1988 to be identified as the author of this
work. All rights reserved. No part of this publication may be repro-
duced, stored in a retrieval system or transmitted in any form, or by
any means (electronic, mechanical, or otherwise) without the prior
written permission of both the copyright
owners and the publisher.

Some of the material in this book is adapted from articles
originally published in the Oldie and the Big Issue.

A CIP catalogue record for this book
is available from the British Library.

ISBN: 978-1-78072-254-2

Cover image copyright:
Getty // Jeff J Mitchell, image ref: 96492886

Endpaper images copyright:
Louise Haywood-Schiefer (top left & top right)
Tom Miller (top centre & bottom right)

Printed at CPI Group (UK) Ltd, Croydon CR0 4YY

For Gill, Dino, Raymond and in memory of Candy.

CONTENTS

Introduction

"Crosswords and Sudoku will help but the best way to avoid dementia is to take up ballroom dancing."

It was in the spring after George died of lung cancer and vascular dementia that I went to a conference organised by the Alzheimer's Society and one of the lecturers gave that advice. It might be a rather feeble excuse, but I left school when I was fourteen, and although I've sometimes read the first crossword clue I've never attempted to think of an answer. For a start, I didn't have the Latin, and nor could I have understood the puns or learnt the tricks, both skills I've been told are essential for completing even quite simple crosswords. As for Sudoku, I'd rather waste my

11

time looking at Facebook or Freecycle. But ballroom dancing?

For some reason, I assumed learning to dance would be easy and I signed up for a twelve-week course. When I left school I got a job in Murray's Cabaret Club as a showgirl and had to shimmy across the small stage in rather skimpy costumes. I thought this would give me a head start. But no. Ballroom dancing is difficult. That is why it is so effective at warding off the ageing process. As a recent study from the Einstein College of Medicine in New York has shown, ballroom demands a particular form of coordination, which rewires the cerebral cortex and the hippocampus. These bits of the brain are remarkably plastic, but they will only become active again if they are properly used. Shimmying isn't enough.

The course I had signed up for provided a teacher for the class plus a professional partner for every client. Most of the partners were young men in their twenties and came from countries like Romania, Italy or Sri Lanka where, unlike in England, dancing is considered a skill and not necessarily sissy. However, I'd quickly spotted Raymond – both English and a pensioner, he was the only one with a balding head and a bus pass. I'd decided I wouldn't feel so self-conscious dancing "in hold" with someone closer to my age. I made a good choice; Ray is a former world champion.

We learnt and practised a different dance for three weeks. The list began with the slow foxtrot and the cha-cha-cha and having passed through six more dances, it ended up with the Viennese waltz and the salsa. By the time we got back to the waltz and cha-cha-cha again, what with holidays and each term lasting fifteen weeks, I had forgotten most of what I'd learnt.

Raymond, seeing how dispirited I was, offered to take me to tea dances instead, so I'd have the opportunity to practise all the dances in one session.

I wish that I'd started ballroom and going to tea dances when George was still alive. In the last two years of his life, I was usually stressed, and often angry with him. I would forget all the useful advice I'd been given about how to cope with his condition and I was snappy and spiteful. But here's what Dr Joseph Coyle says in the *New England Journal of Medicine*: "Dancing reduces stress and depression."

It would have been better than Xanax.

Coyle goes on to say that dancing will increase your serotonin levels; it is known as the "happiness hormone" and studies have shown that a lack of it increases irritability, aggressiveness and sleep disorders. He also talks about it exercising our cognitive processes. And then there's the music. Most of it dates from the first 60 years of the twentieth century:

13

Sinatra, Crosby, Ella, singing songs by Cole Porter, Irving Berlin, Rogers and Hammerstein. Who could ask for anything more?

Some doctors are making very ambitious claims for the Argentine tango and are using it to treat problems ranging from Alzheimer's and Parkinson's disease to phobias and marital breakdowns. My marriage to George nearly broke up several times; instead of rows and tears perhaps we should have hurried down to the local milonga. There's one in Hammersmith twice a week. But would it have halted the progression of his illness? In fact, he was lucky in that his lung cancer overtook the dementia and he died while the latter was still in its fairly early stages. But he would have enjoyed the "close embrace" the tango demands.

Even people at a fairly advanced stage of dementia will normally respond to warmth, touch and sound. Once a month I help out at an afternoon event organised by Kensington and Chelsea Age UK. It's called My Memories Café. The "service users", in other words the people with dementia, are picked up from their homes and taken to a church where tea, cakes, sausage rolls and grapes are laid out on long tables. There's always an activity and the most popular ones involve music. At Christmas time we sing carols. A month ago we sang along accompanied by one man playing the keyboard and another with a mic helping us remember the words.

If you were the only girl in the world... "Isn't that the most beautiful love song ever written?" the keyboard man asked us. We nodded, held hands and swayed to "I'll Be with You in Apple Blossom Time". When we got to the closing number, "Do the Hokey Cokey", although not many could stand up and shake it all about, arms were waved and most people joined in and were smiling. One woman told me how she met her husband at the Hammersmith Palais. She said she always watches *Strictly* and was delighted to hear that, perhaps because of that programme, ballroom and Latin (the other kind) have become very popular.

If, like me, you have type 2 diabetes, your chances of developing Alzheimer's may be increased. That's the bad news. The good news is that exercise and weight loss might counteract this. Since I've been dancing my cheeks have sunk and I've gone down a dress size. Still, what's much more important is the fun I am having.

STRICTLY
TEA DANCE

Chapter 1

"I said I'd dance with you, not *for* you" said Raymond.

But this is my first tea dance and I am nervous, very nervous. Although it's only a waltz, at which I am not too bad, I am leaning on him and gripping his hand.

We are in Shoreditch Town Hall, a grade two imposing building near Liverpool Street. A statue of Progress sits on the front and inside there are stained-glass windows, Doric columns and an ornate balcony. From a high-coved ceiling hang chandeliers. At one end of the large rectangular ballroom is a big stage with a massive sound system that rather dwarfs our compère, Malcolm (professional name, Mr Wonderful). Malcolm is a smallish, round, cheerful man from Goa, India. His partner, Janet, is a former senior champion.

All around the room are tables and chairs. We sit down after our waltz and Raymond tells me, and not for the first time, that I must find my own balance and relax a bit.

18

"Nobody is watching you," he says.

This isn't strictly true. The entrance fee is a modest £5 and some of the ladies have just come for the tea and cakes and to watch the dancers. They must be wondering why Raymond is dancing with me. Being an ex-champion, he is of course a brilliant dancer.

Mr Wonderful announces the next dance. It's a paso doble which I haven't learnt. Anna, a fantastic, young, slim, dancer has spotted Raymond and comes over.

"Do you mind?" she says to me, as Raymond enthusiastically jumps to his feet.

"Oh, please," I reply. I realise I am quite enjoying myself. I don't mind sitting on my own; the atmosphere is friendly and the music is the dance music of the 40s and 50s that I grew up with.

The next dance is a "snowball". It starts with just one couple on the floor, then Mr Wonderful says "change partners" and they separate and each chooses a new partner. We change partners every few minutes and soon the floor is crowded with about 50 couples. Most of us change partners about five times. I always say I'm a beginner but some of the men are even more of a beginner than I am. The "snowball" is quite chatty; you change partners so often you don't have time to perform complicated steps. It's more of a shuffle and an exchange of names.

"George," says one man when I ask him.

"Same as my late husband," I reply, and as I have just stepped on his toe I add swankily and placatingly, "He was the jazz singer, George Melly."

He can't have been as impressed as he appeared to be as he came up to me later and asked me to repeat George's last name. But Mr Wonderful is impressed. Raymond has introduced me to him as the widow of, etc.

"Great," says Mr Wonderful. "I must play lots of jive music for you."

In fact, I've noticed that Raymond never stands up for a jive. I don't think he likes to get too hot – well, he is 65 – and over tea and chocolate cake – Raymond eats my bit too – I learn that he is a great-grandfather. His eldest daughter, Rita, had daughter Cyd at eighteen and she in turn at seventeen has just had a son, little Leo.

Raymond has now finished all the cake, we've sorted our families and rubbished David Cameron, so it's time to tango.

A very friendly dance, as Raymond puts it. To get into position I have to push my "centre", which is halfway between my flat chest and my not-so-flat stomach into Raymond's centre. Then I have to flex my knees so that I am almost sitting on one half of his lap. The hold is different too. My left hand is pushed up into his armpit with my thumb in front and my fingers stuck out at a right angle to his back.

Raymond tells me that the Argentine tango is even more friendly, with the lady reaching her left hand round her partner's back to rest on his left shoulder, or even on the back of his neck. Sounds to me more like hugging than dancing.

Even with our "centres" up close, all this proximity isn't sexual at all, but it's warm and cosy, rather like having one of my dogs curled up on my lap.

It's the last waltz and I'm thrilled because I haven't fallen over or made a fool of myself. Even when I messed up a slow foxtrot it didn't seem to matter.

Raymond walks me to Liverpool Street, taking my arm as we go down the stairs. "Call me old-fashioned" is something he often says, and although I am quite capable of putting on my own coat, I don't mind being helped.

It's six years since George died and I thought that my family, friends and dogs were all I needed to feel sane and whole. I now realise that music and dancing help too.

MY DOUBLE-DECKER

Chapter 2

Someone once told me that she had enough friends to fill a double-decker bus and she hadn't room for any more. She was only in her thirties when she said that. I remembered this remark the other day and I thought, she's now in her late seventies, the same as me. The likelihood is that some of them have got off the bus because of a quarrel, or a move to Australia, or they have fallen off the bus: Aids, cancer or a heart attack. Well, if she has lost as many friends as I have, she might well consider going to tea dances and finding some new ones, which is what I've done. This happens when Ray doesn't come with me and I have to go on my own.

Pam is one of my new friends. She had been at George's last concert, a charity event in aid of Dementia UK. I had been pushing him in his wheel-chair, so Pam recognised me and came over to chat.

Pam is tall, elegant, a great dancer, and looks to be in her early sixties. But as she has a great-grandchild and assuming she didn't get married at fourteen, she must be in her seventies. One thing seems to be true about the women who go dancing: they all look much younger than their years. Last month at Battersea Town Hall the compère announced that the woman dancing a speedy quickstep was celebrating her 100th birthday.

Then there's Gill. Aged 58, looks 35 and comes from the valleys. It's important as you get older to make some younger friends to fill up the bus. Grandchildren aren't always to hand or willing, and some of us need help with modern technology. Nor do we wish to sound like that old judge who asked "What exactly is a beetle?"

Gill has taken me under her wing. Men flock to lead her onto the dance floor and when they politely return her to our table she says, "Now my friend would like to dance." I refuse to be embarrassed and I'm suitably grateful. I'm reminded of that Patrick Hamilton novel in which two men spot a couple of girls they want to pick up and the dominant male says, "I'll have the blonde, you can have the other one."

Sometimes after a tea dance we collect my dogs from home and go for a walk in the park. We discuss, rather disrespectfully, the various men who've been in our lives. Gill's last boyfriend used to dress up in her underwear. Gill is tiny; the boyfriend was six foot with a big stomach. Having swapped a few juicy tales, we move on to our jobs. Gill works as a volunteer for a children's charity. I work in the visitors' centre at a local prison.

We quite often sit at a table with Scotty. He's been given that nickname because after being bombed three times during the Blitz he was evacuated from the East End to Scotland. The explosions also made him deaf and sometimes he struggles with Gill's Welsh accent, but then so do I. Scottie doesn't do much ballroom – he's more of a Latin man, although jiving is his speciality. Like many people, he makes the wrong assumption that as George was a jazz singer, I must be a fabulous jiver. I'm not. In his later years George only sang at concerts – no prospect of jiving there. And in those wonderful early days when he sang in small scruffy jazz clubs, he preferred me to stand at the foot of the stage and gaze up at him admiringly. All the girlfriends and wives did the same.

Clearly the women who come to tea dances, some of them in their eighties, weren't hampered by such partners. They're so skilful at "American spins" and "chicken walks" that I think they must have been just the right age to have learnt their steps from American GIs during and after the war. But Scotty often pulls me to my feet if the compère is playing a slow jive like "Hit the Road Jack", and so far I've managed not to fall over. I like talking to him too. In common with a lot of deaf people (and men in general), he's better at storytelling than listening. I have learnt that he was once a taxi driver and has a daughter who lost both legs in the July 7th bombings. She was a winner in the Paralympics and has just had a baby.

Raymond is on the front of the bus with my other best friends. Ray is an accomplished flirt and does a very sexy rumba. In spite of these attributes, we have a purely platonic relationship. There are advantages in getting older – somehow it's easier to have a heterosexual male friend when sex is not an issue, and anyway, in many respects Ray is like my gay friends. He will discuss clothes, make-up and hairstyles, the best boiler and other domestic issues.

For many people getting old is awful. I'm quite aware that I'm lucky. I have enough money and my bus is full of great friends.

THE SHOW GOES ON
AND ON AND ON

Chapter 3

Raymond and I have come to Blackpool to watch the Latin and Ballroom National Dance Championships. He is very excited about it. "You won't see much better dancing than this."

And ever the optimist, he has also expressed the hope that it might improve my technique. I have come because I was brought up in the olden days when women were taught to please the opposite sex and to agree enthusiastically to any plan. Also I like a jaunt away from home.

In the foyer of the Winter Gardens, a beautiful art deco building, we meet up with John and Christine, friends who like me are learning to dance; in a reversal from the usual it's John who is keen and Christine who goes along with it. She tells me that while John is learning the leader's steps, her attention wanders and, sitting on the windowsill, she stares out until called to attention by her understandably annoyed teacher. It's good having Chris to gossip with; we criticise the dresses while Ray and John assess the dancing.

"Dresses" doesn't adequately describe what they

30

are wearing. For the ballroom, the women wear long floating chiffon garments with fishing line threaded through the hems to make the skirts stand out and undulate. Sometimes the sleeves have streamers attached to them – not a good look – or wide floating bits of material. These are meant to make the arms appear graceful, but quite often the material floats up and stretches across the face of the dancers, temporarily blinding them, and making them more likely to crash into other couples. They remind me of Magritte paintings.

When Magritte was thirteen his mother committed suicide. He saw her carried into the house on a stretcher; she had been fished out of a canal and her dress had blown over her face. This image obsessed him, and he used it frequently. In one of his paintings that George used to own (he sold it to buy a stretch of river), a pair of lovers, their faces concealed with material, are unable to kiss or make contact. In another, one couple are gracefully dancing, but another have tumbled to the floor. Magritte named this painting *The Clumsy Dancer*.

Chris and I have gone to the ladies, our main purpose being to mingle with the competitors. The Latins are in there getting ready for their next dance; beautiful young women are touching up their spray tan, fixing inch-long eyelashes and gluing diamond-like stones to their faces. While the foxtrotters' and waltzers' dresses are soft and flowing, the Latin dancers' outfits resemble birds of paradise: they glitter and are sexy and sharp, with bright shining colours.

We stay till the results of the Amateurs are announced and the cups presented. It's time to go back to our hotel and I'm beginning to dread tomorrow. We don't get to bed till two and there are lectures scheduled for ten in the morning. Lectures about ballroom dancing?

And then, in a blink, here we are in the queue – me suffering from a lack of coffee. As usual ballroom fanatics have a lot to say to each other. "It's only an opinion," says Ray who had disagreed with the judge's choice of the Latin winner. He overhears a young man talking and asks, "Are you looking for a partner?'

"Yes."

"Ballroom or Latin?"

"Latin."

"I know a good sixteen-year-old."

"That's a bit young."

"And a good 25-year-old but she's ballroom. Do you do ballroom?"

"Only since February."

"That's a no then."

We file politely into the Spanish Room where three

hours of lectures are about to begin. I'm rather sleepy but wake up as the lecture begins with Mike Daniels, a former champion, spinning round the floor. Three of the lectures are given by couples, dance partners who are also married. Marital strife is rather obvious. Apparently it's well known that couples who never normally exchange a cross word fight like Taylor and Burton once on the dance floor.

The rest of the day is for exploring Blackpool. Perhaps because the sun is shining and the sky and sea are a clear blue I think Blackpool is a magical city and why would one go anywhere else for a holiday? We climb on a tram to Fleetwood, a town ten miles north of Blackpool on the Fylde peninsula. (Rather annoyingly I've forgotten my bus pass; Raymond never forgets his.) Fleetwood was once an important deep-sea fishing port but the industry was destroyed in the 70s by the cod war. We head for the market; I need some knitting wool, not something easily found in London. As usual Raymond needs fish and chips. One café opposite the market has an enticing sign: Pensioner's special: Fish and chips, cod or hake, cup of tea, bread and butter all inclusive £4.

Tonight, the last night, is the Professional Finals. The competitors are not the only ones who dress up. I have and so have the judges. They are dressed for a red carpet night. Some of the women are in long black or crimson velvet dresses, bare shoulders, hair in French pleats. They all look elegant. The men wear dinner jackets; so do most of the former champions, including Raymond. He explains they're keen to keep up the standards.

The last cup has been presented, "God Save the Queen" is played and we all stumble to our feet, even me. Gone are the days when it was played at the end of a film or a play and George and I would stay firmly on our bums.

EN SUITE?

Chapter 4

"I'm a performance poet," says the receptionist at the Margate hotel. "This is my website." He scribbles the address down on a bit of scrap paper.

"Perhaps we could have the keys to our rooms and look at it later?" I say. I don't want to be rude but I'm quite anxious to see my room and find out if it has an en suite. I've arrived in Margate with Raymond for an evening dance at the Winter Gardens ballroom arranged by Mr Wonderful. Raymond has found us this hotel which is only £27 a night, so it's on the cards that the nearest loo will be down a passage. Back in the 60s when I went on tour with George, I don't think en suite existed in the sort of hotels that jazz musicians stayed in, but that was then and I was in my 20s and didn't have to get up in the night.

In the reception area is a very large radio dating from the 40s. It's finished in light walnut veneer with a beige-brown fabric cover over the speaker. The material has a glistening gold-coloured thread running through it and a tuning wheel on one side of the glass indicator panel showing the stations, including

Hilversum, Brussels, Prague, Luxembourg and the like. Along the base of the panel are about a dozen chunky cream-coloured, cube-shaped buttons, each about the size of a marshmallow, for selecting the radio's various functions. David, the performance poet, comes from behind the desk and leads the way up the maze of stairs and corridors. We stop at each point of interest: on one landing there is a pinball machine and on another a display cabinet stuffed with ancient photos and pewter award mugs; but will there be an en suite?

Yes! There is! My room is small but spotless; there are three hangers in the wardrobe, a TV and a bedside light. The latter doesn't seem to work but after dancing till ten that is hardly going to matter.

For some reason Raymond wants to go for a paddle, but I need lunch. Margate has fish and chips or pizza to offer. We settle for the usual fish and chips which I haven't had so often since they were wrapped in the *Sunday Dispatch*. Raymond goes the whole hog and has sliced white bread and butter and a mug of strong tea with his. We stop at the Turner gallery where there is a rather disappointing exhibition and then Raymond goes for his paddle with the bottoms of his trousers rolled up. I feel I missed a photo opportunity there.

After a bracing walk along the seafront past Frank's

Night Club (closed and boarded up), ten-pin bowling (open and packed), numerous pawn shops also doing good business, Raymond ("call me old-fashioned") takes my arm and we cross the road for tea and cakes in a dainty tea shop. I consider broaching the subject of our "issue" with the Argentine tango. It was either an issue or a problem, I'm not quite sure of the difference; I don't think it was a row but I did call him a pig.

It happened one week at my regular tango lesson. There are six of us learning and six professional partners, of whom Raymond is one. Usually I dance with Raymond but that night, when I completely failed to notice him offering me the back of his knee for a "gancho", he became impatient with me and so I called him a pig. At that point our instructor said we could change partners, and Raymond seized the opportunity to dump me.

So, hoping the chocolate cake has worked its magic on Raymond's sweet tooth, I begin. "Raymond, I could write 50 lines saying 'I must not call my teacher a pig', or I could just say sorry."

"If being lippy does anything at all to improve your tango," he replies, "so be it."

Back at the hotel I change into my skinny black Jasper Conran jeans and a grey silk top covered in sequins. From the outside, the Winter Gardens ballroom looks a little sad, but inside it's dazzling. It was built at a cost of £26,000 in 1911 in the neo-Grecian style. In the early 1920s, performers like Carrie Tubb, Harry Dearth, Pavlova and Madame Melba were all engaged to play in the elegant concert hall. Then, during the Second World War it acted as a receiving station for some of the 46,000 troops who landed at Margate from Dunkirk. There were also concerts for the troops on Sundays and "brighten-up dances" every Thursday and Saturday. After the war Webster Booth and Anne Ziegler, Stan Laurel and Oliver Hardy, and Vera Lynn all appeared there; so did the Beatles and indeed George in the 60s.

In the ballroom there is a large revolving glitter ball competing with my sequin top for the bling effect; there's a bar and a bay window giving an 180-degree view of the sea. Lots of familiar faces from other tea dances have come: there's the couple we call Cuddles because even in the jive they stay wrapped round each other, a young girl I call Druggy because she told Raymond that she flies to and from Mexico once a month, and a man I call Uppy because he gives off an upper-class vibe. I was quite wrong about the latter: we chat at the bar and I realise he's from Essex, but unlike me hadn't been given elocution lessons.

It's last waltz time – the Tennessee waltz – a sad song about a girl whose best friend goes off with her lover. Before I had even kissed a boy I identified with that pathetic creature.

Back at the hotel, the ancient night porter who lets us in has got the old radio on; the light it gives off is like that from a real living-room fire. The familiar medium-wave sound, muffled and complete with buzzes and clicks as it fades in and out, is friendly and reassuring. And it's playing "After You've Gone", one of my favourites; I rather wish it were George singing. That would have been perfect.

BLACK EYES and BANDAGES

Chapter 5

Why am I standing at the bus stop with a bandaged leg, wearing sunglasses in a queue of women and all of us waiting for a man?

Well, I'm not waiting for the 52 – I'm in Battersea Town Hall with Raymond and the bus stop is the name of the next dance. We ladies all queue up on one side of the dance floor and as each man approaches he takes the lady at the front of the queue, whizzes her round the floor and then leaves her at the back of the queue.

The ladies all ask about my bandage. I explain that on the way here with Raymond, I stepped off the train and fell down the gap between it and the platform.

The men all ask about the sunglasses; one says, "Are you in disguise?"

"No, I just forgot to take them off."

One man seems to be doing a waltz, although Mr Wonderful is definitely playing a quickstep – "Zing Went the Strings of My Heart"; another tall, flashy dancer is trying to make me do a running spin turn. I explain I've only learnt the spin turn without the running bit. Mr Flashy ignores me and has only himself to blame when I fall over his feet and we crash into another couple.

I'm extremely relieved when the bus stop is over and I'm back at the table.

"Why didn't you tell me I still had my sunglasses on?" I ask Raymond.

"I thought you might have pink eye," he replies. He gets up and brings me back a cup of tea with two sugars. "For the shock," he says.

He'd seen me disappear onto the line at the station and had been more frightened than I was; and, being rather squeamish, had looked away when the station's first-aid man had tipped Dettol onto my leg wound and mopped up the blood. He also gives me his bit of cake, and seeing he has a very sweet tooth, this is more than generous.

A man called Peter that I recognise from the last tea dance comes very very slowly towards me. Last time we danced, well, not exactly danced, just moved sedately round the floor, he told me that he was 82 last birthday and his mother looks after him. Well, either his mother was sixteen when she gave birth or he has mild dementia.

Because of George I'm quite comfortable with dementia. He also had many fantasies. One was that he had been asked to play Jesus Christ in a new

Hollywood blockbuster. Another was that Manny Shinwell, an important member of Attlee's post-war Labour government and dead for 25 years, was building several workmen's cottages in our garden.

Peter and I have finished our stately shuffle and Mr Wonderful has announced a slow foxtrot, "I'd Like to Get You on a Slow Boat to China".

"Face your fears," says Raymond, leading me on to the floor. "And please try to remember some of what I've taught you. Take longer steps; your legs start from under your armpits. Release your weight. And lift your arms from your elbows, we don't need your shoulders, and imagine you are going to hug a large oak tree, extend your neck away from your partner. You have a long neck, so use it."

By the time we've danced the last waltz, "Beware my Foolish Heart", I'm beginning to feel the effects of my fall: my knee hurts, my side aches but as I admire the stoics I don't complain and limp up Lavender Hill to the station. The train is full but a young Asian man gives me his seat.

THE
CEILIDH

Chapter 6

In the last few months I've been to tea dances in the Tower Ballroom in Blackpool, the Royal Opera House, Shoreditch Town Hall, Battersea Town Hall and the O2 Centre in Finchley road. I've been to supper dances in a five-star hotel in Majorca, a small village in Essex (black tie optional) and the Guild Hall, Cambridge (black tie, please). But I had the most fun in a Catholic church hall in Acton. Well, it's not every day you can jive underneath a huge portrait of the last Pope.

It wasn't just the Pope – it became quite obvious that although advertised as a tea dance (two till five), we were about to enjoy a ceilidh, (in other words a Celtic shindig). The DJ, Bob, is wearing a black cowboy hat and is dressed in black jeans and a black T-shirt. Although a large man, he exudes rhythm. He plays what can best be described as country and western with its roots in Ulster, alternating with popular Irish songs. We change into our dance shoes, but we are the only ones to bother and people stare.

At the long bar the Guinness is flowing and Raymond is soon in a very good mood. Ray learnt to dance when he was twelve at his secondary modern, where an enterprising headmaster told the boys it was a good way to meet girls. He made them bryl-creem their hair and wear a clean shirt. Not only did Ray meet lots of girls, he had a talent, and when he was 24 he won the world championship for Latin and the 10-Dance championship. Ray is now in his sixties but something called muscle memory has meant that he hasn't forgotten anything. Of course I'm lucky to have him as a partner, but he is very strict. "Did you do a heel turn? I thought not"; "you can't have forgotten the tango chase, you only learnt it last week!"

I once extracted a compliment from him: "that was nearly good."

Happily, the Guinness and the atmosphere have had an effect: Raymond is beaming and has stopped complaining.

The tempo of the music in "When Irish Eyes are Smiling" is like a slow Viennese waltz or a fast ordinary one so we do a cha-cha-cha. The DJ plays "Home on the Range" – it's hard to know what dance we are meant to be doing so we do a sexy rumba. A woman clearly impressed by Ray's hip movements leads him on to the floor. I'm left sitting under a large sign that says "Do not stand on the tables", but Raymond is not the only one enjoying the Guinness and I'm soon doing a sort of jig with a man from Belfast. At least that's what I think he said.

Twenty people form a circle and everyone takes their turn in the centre to dance. Raymond does his John Travolta imitation from *Pulp Fiction*. You couldn't say there's much physical resemblance; there's the age difference and Ray's lack of hair for a start, but Ray has all the confidence of a person who knows they are really good at something, and there is much clapping as he twists away. One lady does the Charleston and a portly gentleman attempts a Russian folk dance. Not wishing to be pulled into the centre, I make for the bar and buy a round for our table. Ray has decided that as long as the music is slow enough it will suit the Argentine tango. "Keep it simple," I beg as we take to the floor. I haven't been learning long, but it's not appropriate to come over all shy so I drape myself round Ray and he leads me through barridas, ganchos and ochos.

One or two women have asked Ray if he will teach them the Argentine and on the way home he says he can feel his ego swelling and will I please tell him if he's getting too big for his boots. Well, in 45 years I never had much success in cutting George down to size, I'm pleased to have a go at such an enjoyable task.

A NEW TEACHER

Chapter 7

I had known for some time that I had to find a new dance teacher. Raymond had become so popular as a partner and a teacher that I could no longer rely on him to take me to tea dances. He was happy to give me a weekly lesson but what with his children, his grandchild, his great-grandson, his other students, his ex-wife and his girlfriend now back from Hong Kong, my nose was out of joint. And there were problems with his teaching methods; he taught me steps – or tried to – that nobody but him could dance. He once spent three lessons trying to teach me a double reverse spin. I had written down the instructions in a note-book so that I could practice at home. Once home, these instructions made no sense to me:

R back, com t l heel t r side x left in front of r.

He used to say that he was "trying to take me up a level" and even once suggested that I should enter for some medals. They might call them medals, but I call them exams and if I have got into my seventies without taking an exam since the 11 plus I am not going to start now, even if they are called bronze, silver and gold.

In spite of the friends I had made at tea dances – and Gill was always ready to come with me – it was a dismal experience going without Ray. I knew that I had to become proactive and tackle the problem. I sent him an email explaining that I wanted to find a teacher who would be able to come to social dances with me and I was sure we would still be friends. He replied, "Whilst my head can understand, my heart doesn't want to listen. I'm a bit stunned, but not to worry, I'll process it all."

What with Google and the popularity of *Strictly*, it is easy to find dance classes. After very little searching, I found one in Holland Park, five minutes from where I live in Shepherd's Bush. There was a two-hour class divided into beginners and intermediate followed by an hour and a half of social dancing. I decided to start off in beginners until I found my confidence. It was lacking partly because of Raymond's inability to deliver any form of praise. I don't blame him. It's not easy learning to dance at any age, let alone mine. I have no muscle memory for the 'six quick twinkle', the 'curved feather' or the 'brush tap'. But put me on a bike and I could still ride without my hands on the handlebars. Raymond has got all that muscle memory from his years of training. I think he only put up with me because we became such good friends. Such good friends that on the trip to Blackpool where we'd gone to watch the championships, we were able to share a room without any embarrassment. Raymond always describes himself as a super scrimper and he had found the room on the seafront minutes from the Winter Gardens for £30 a night. I was a little worried before I saw the room. I had been dreading one of those twin rooms where the beds are separated only by a minute plastic bedside table. But this room was perfect, almost L-shaped in design with my single bed tucked discreetly into a corner almost out of sight of Raymond's large double. That might not sound very gentlemanly of him but he is almost six foot compared to my five foot five.

I have often shared with women on holiday and there are the usual worries about snoring and going to the loo in the middle of the night. I remembered that when I was five and at a Catholic boarding school, I once became very ill and was taken to sleep in Sister Magdalena's room. When she took off her wimple before going to bed I saw with some horror her neatly shaved head. She then removed her voluminous habit and got into her equally voluminous night clothes without ever exposing an inch of flesh.

With a man, sharing when you are not romantically involved brings other worries. In Blackpool I put my nightdress on over my tights and pants and took them off while decently covered. It all came quite naturally to me. I come from an age when women were quite shy of exposing their bodies. I never saw my mother or any of my friends naked.

Going to the lavatory in the morning in the en suite which was so en suite as to almost be in the room was a worry. Here Ray's appetite for the full English breakfast (included in the price) and my small spoonful of muesli solved the problem. I had plenty of time to myself before Raymond returned, having finally finished his scrambled egg, sausage, bacon, tinned tomatoes and fried bread.

Now that I was without Ray it was time to be bold and check out Holland Park. The first time I went I saw it was a completely different crowd from the tea dance set. For a start they were all much younger. That made sense – the class took place in the evening. Most young people are working during tea dance time or if they are one of the sixteen per cent of young people unable to find work they don't have the five or six pounds to go waltzing, let alone the inclination.

I didn't enjoy myself very much but I knew that if I wanted to keep dancing, and I did, I would have to persevere with finding the right set-up and the right teacher. So the next week I went to Holland Park again. I was pleased I decided to stay in the beginners' group because we had one or two professional partners to help us. Dancing with men who are also learning, and sometimes have two left feet, isn't much fun. A nice slow rumba was playing and a man called Dino came over to help me.

"I can't do the spot turn."

"Yes, you can. Look at me. Have your weight on your right foot. Look to your right and step to your right with your left foot. Look again to your right, swivel on your standing leg, change weight, look at me again. You've turned 360 degrees."

It was quite simple – I did it.

Halfway through the social bit of the evening I decided I'd had enough of being brave and started to take off my dancing shoes. Dino came over and asked me why I was leaving. "Stay and practise your spot turns," he said.

I gave the excuse that I needed to get home to my dogs and soon we were exchanging dog stories and photos. He had found his dog, a tiny puppy, in the dustbin. Then because I was recovering from bronchitis and had got out of breath dancing a quickstep with him, we got on to smoking. I started when I passed the 11 plus. Those were the days when even doctors smoked while listening to your chest and Craven A were advertised as being "so good for the throat".

Although I gave up when I was 49, 38 years of heavy smoking had damaged my lungs. Dino told me that his mother who was the same age as me had had two heart bypasses and still smoked.

I knew then that if Dino gave lessons I had found my new teacher. How do you find out if someone is a teacher? Is it a rude question? I decided to risk it. "Dino, do you teach?"

"I'll teach *you*, darling, it would be a pleasure."

In spite of darling this and darling that, Dino is camp but not gay. I knew this because along with the puppy photos there were several of his girlfriend Dora, who, like him, is Greek.

We swapped phone numbers, not emails – Dino is computer illiterate and within a week we had fixed up my first lesson and also arranged to go to a Saturday dance so that Dora, who works in the week, could come too. I was very happy and realised how miserable I had been about not having a dance teacher.

Also I was looking forward to the dance cruise that I was going on with Gill. She is even more efficient than me and as I had never been on a cruise before I left her to make all the arrangements. All I knew was that there would be dancing from seven until midnight every evening and that when I came back I had someone to go dancing with.

THE CRUISE

Chapter 8

On a *QE2* cruise, if you are a solo traveller, gay in search of a friend or struggling with your alcohol addiction, you will be well catered for. "Friends of Dorothy" met at five in the Commodore's Club. In the days when Judy Garland was a gay icon, "Are you a friend of Dorothy?" was how you found out if another person was homosexual. "Friends of Bill W" also met at five but in the Admiral's Lounge. Bill W was an American who co-founded Alcoholics Anonymous. Bad luck if you were gay in need of a friend and also trying not to hit the bottle. Perhaps you could go to the venues on alternate nights? As a solo, presumably a straight solo, there was a solo travellers' coffee and cookie morning and twice a week a solo travellers' lunch.

Gill and I didn't really belong in any of these categories; we were just there for the dancing. So on our first night we had a quick dinner: Roast Rack of Lamb, with Roast Potatoes, Ratatouille, Green Beans and a Rosemary Jus. We skipped the Hot Grand Marnier

Soufflé with Custard Sauce, put on our new silver shoes and went to the Queen's ballroom.

Nearly all the other travellers must have been still unpacking because we had the six dance hosts to ourselves. None of them came anywhere near the standard of Raymond or Dino, and the one from Arizona had a strange way of waltzing. Everyone knows you close your feet on the third step, but not in America. "Don't close your feet," said Robert from Arizona, so I didn't and we danced a slow foxtrot in waltz timing.

I never met anyone at tea dances who wanted to be a cruise ship host. I was told that their duties didn't end on the dance floor – they had to escort the ladies round the ports when the boat docked, they had to have a vast wardrobe of evening and casual clothes and they mustn't sweat too much. They mustn't sleep with the passengers or show favouritism. If they did they would be turned off the boat and have to buy their own passage home. Some companies demanded to see a bank balance to make sure a potential host had sufficient funds for this. It's rumoured that before the pill there were so many paternity suits that many companies only employed gay hosts. This was no longer a qualification; it was hard to know what was. Gill nicknamed one of the hosts "Mr Pastry" and she decided that his only qualification would have been having two feet.

Halfway through the evening, the live orchestra and the hosts went off for a break but there was still piped music so Gill and I danced together. It's possible that we looked a little odd; Gill is a seriously good dancer, and so, although she is five inches shorter than me and size 6 to my size 10, she has to be the leader. The cha-cha-cha became our speciality – we thought waltzing together might look really silly. Back in our room I was rather shattered after five hours' dancing. Not Gill, she knows not only how to wait until the cruise price comes down to what a weekend in a cheap B&B in Swansea would cost, but, how to get upgraded. An hour later we had been transported to a room further from the chug-chug-chug of the engine and with an outside balcony. This is Gill's fourth cruise and she has reached gold status, which gives her extra benefits like welcome champagne and invitations to the captain's parties.

We could have spent the next morning learning bridge, attending a watercolour class, or at the Golden Lion pub for morning trivia or playing table tennis. Not wanting to do any of those things or even attend Kate Adie's lecture, we went line dancing. I used to go line dancing before I got serious and took up ballroom, mostly because I love country and western. I remembered how important it is to position yourself on the floor. You usually turn to face one of the four walls, so it's no good being at the front or back. You need an expert in front of you, behind you and on either side of you. What I hadn't learnt in Shepherd's Bush Village Hall was how to stay upright when the *QE2* began to battle with the Atlantic. The waves were impressive, ten metres high, the purser told us, as we bucketed through a force 11 gale. The cha-cha-cha lesson that followed was even more challenging, even the hosts were falling about.

But I loved the movement of the boat, especially the feeling at night of being rocked to sleep. No one seemed that worried by it, although there were quite a few Zimmer frames and wheelchairs. Talk about an aging population – given that there were 2000 people on board and at least half of them over 60, surely there must sometimes be a death on these cruises? And if so, what do they do with the body?

Gill was one of the youngest of the dancing crowd. I think there was a younger set that we didn't see much of because they ate in the Lido and went to the disco. Anyone could eat in the Britannia where we did but it was silver service and you had to be suitably dressed. Formal evenings meant dinner jackets and elegant dresses; informal meant just a jacket and cocktail dresses. No tank tops, sandals or jeans anywhere on the boat after six.

For some reason I thought that the *QE2* would be

similar to the huge boats that go up and down the Nile and that the restaurant would be a better version of a steak house. Quite wrong: the restaurant is a beautiful art deco room with good but slightly elaborate food and clever waiters. They remembered that we didn't like ice in our water and although I wanted only one glass of wine, I wanted it before I even sat down. At dinner we always had a table to ourselves, while at breakfast and lunch we often had to share. This was not a problem for Gill, as she is kind and can listen. Perhaps this skill is enhanced by her job, which involves listening to sad stories and being able to judge the probability of suicide, self-harm, abuse, etc.

At breakfast I was always too stunned by the lack of the double espresso that I'm used to at home to say anything. But Gill is never at a loss for words, (I think that's due to being Welsh). She would have been a gift to the diplomatic service. I only once saw her speechless and almost cross; a woman with whom we were sharing a table told us how much she hated cruising. She said she was only on the boat so she could spend two days shopping in Fort Lauderdale. She then informed us that her daughter who lived in London had to take taxis everywhere because of the dangers on public transport, "Pickpockets and you know what else". Gill and I both got up and left realising we might be getting into "I am not a racist,

DIANA MELLY

but..." territory. She was the only unpleasant person we met. Going on cruises doesn't seem like a posh thing to do. Most of our fellow travellers were "room at the top", working-class people who had made good. There was often talk of the tin baths and outside lavvies that their grandparents had had.

The Black and White ball was the first themed event. Gill wore a vintage white satin dress and I wore a black silk one that Jasper Conran had designed and given me in 1983. Recent events and dancing had meant that I had lost a lot of weight, rather too much, in fact, but at least I could get into the dress. My local dry cleaners had cunningly added some sleeves so my wobbly bat wings were not on show.

Sitting behind us on that first night were two men, both wearing wedding rings, who usually danced together. They were there again on the ball night and Gill decided that we should introduce ourselves. "They look half tidy," she said. The only dance that Paul wouldn't do was the quickstep. So Tim, Paul's husband, and Gill whirled round the room while the ship threw the dancers about and Paul and I swapped our credentials. Paul was from Glasgow and a psychiatrist and Tim was a Londoner and a decorator.

When you are travelling on your own or with

another woman, make a bee-line for the gays; gays like women. I once went down the Nile with my friend Nell and before we had even unpacked we found Tim and Goose. Goose was so called because his surname was Gosling, and three years later they are both still our friends.

One of the many pleasures of taking eight days to go from Southampton to New York is the clocks going back; they did it four times and on those occasions gave us an extra hour in bed. I'd also discovered that room service would bring me a double espresso and there was time for that too. With 1000 staff to 2000 passengers the service was brilliant. Mr Carson of Downton Abbey would be proud of them. They know what you want before you know that you want it. Even your hands are sanitised for you. Outside every public room stands a smiling man ready to squirt the lotion onto your outstretched palms.

I sometimes wondered if we were being somewhat unadventurous. We could have gone home "looking ten years younger", learnt how to fence, how to belly-dance, had a "non-surgical facelift". We did none of those things, but we didn't miss out on the food. Not only were there many different sorts of breakfast: porridge, prunes and pancakes and the sort of full English breakfast that Raymond likes, there was also a three-course lunch. This was followed two hours later by afternoon tea in the Queen's Room. Elegant waiters wearing white server jackets with gold buttons and white gloves served us with cucumber sandwiches, and scones with cream and jam. Discreet piano music added to the 30s atmosphere.

We always went for the early sitting for dinner so that we could have as long as possible on the dance floor. Gill obviously has a very fast metabolism, because in spite of her small size, she always had room for a three-course dinner at six thirty: Deep-Fried Brie in a Mushroom Bread Crust with Cranberry Sauce and Petit Salad, followed by Pan-Seared Peppered Tuna with Carrot Stir-Fry and Rice, then Rum and Raisin and Maple Walnut Ice Cream with Lemon Sorbet and Toffee Sauce. On the way out of the restaurant was a large bowl of chocolates and some oranges, and Gill would fill her dancing-shoe bag with them just in case we needed a midnight snack. Gill usually did.

Lately I had become rather addicted to ice cream and next to the entrance to the Lido was an ice cream machine. It was just like those machines that you hold a cup under and get hot or cold water, except that here you chose a cornet, big or small, and held it under the vanilla or strawberry tap. You took as much as you wanted, and then added a little squirt of chocolate. This made up for having only one glass of wine at night. Well, with all the elements conspiring to wrong-foot you, it wasn't a good idea to be even slightly tipsy. I sometimes had three or four ice creams a day, and they more than made up for the lack of Rioja.

The second formal night had been announced as the London Ball. Gill had bought some packets of stick-on tattoos of various London sights: the Tower of London, Buckingham Palace, etc. I thought if she made an effort it meant I didn't have to. But I did rather wish I'd thought to bring a hideous green dress covered in little pearls I'd bought off eBay. In fact, I would have been outclassed, as one woman wore the full Pearly Queen outfit, hat and feathers and all.

The point of the London Ball is that it's meant to be a jolly Cockney get-together; so if you can't join in, better stay in your cabin. We did the barn dance, the hokey cokey and the Lambeth Walk. Then Gill led one conga snake and Paul Richie, the smooth, handsome crooner, led another. It was a perfect evening.

The following day, the captain told us that we were very near where the *Titanic* had hit the iceberg but not to worry as it wasn't the iceberg season. I didn't; my worries are more domestic in their nature. When the weather had calmed down enough for us not to be blown up against the rails we went up on deck. It's a long way from one end of the boat to the other. If you do a round trip it's one kilometre. Gill often made us do it twice. We stopped every now and then to take photos of each other leaning out over the front pretending to be Kate Winslet before the ship goes down.

One afternoon we went to the sumptuous theatre which had seating for 400 in the stalls, 430 in the dress circle and 20 boxes. A tenor with a passable voice sang an aria from *Rigoletto* and "Besame Mucho", which had been my father's favourite song. He had been in Casablanca during what he called "a good war", which he had spent mostly in the arms of another woman. When he reluctantly returned to Essex where my mother and I were living, he brought with him a photograph of the dark Italian beauty, a bottle of Strega, a Luger and a pair of embroidered slippers which might have fitted me when he was called up some five years previously. He very quickly found a replacement for the Italian. She had a daughter with black ringlets who was smaller, younger and prettier than me. The slippers fitted her perfectly.

Our last themed evening, the Sparkle Ball was a chance to get out the bling. I wore a red chiffon dress covered in tiny mirrors, one of my more successful e-Bay purchases. Gill wore a pink dress with diamanté straps. At dinner I had two glasses of wine – well, it was our last night. We sat at our usual table near Paul and Tim. Janice, our entertainment hostess, announced there would be a *Strictly* competition. The winner would receive a bottle of champagne and all the participants half a bottle. Michael, an Irishman from County Cork, asked Gill to partner him.

I saw Heinz, my favourite host, also had a number on his back, indicating that he was going to be one of the competitors. He stopped at our table and invited me onto my feet. "Oh please, Heinz, no." This would be worse than sitting for the 11 plus. But there comes a moment when it's churlish and bad manners to keep saying no. I sometimes think that occasionally I went to bed with men I didn't really like so as not to seem rude. There were six couples competing, and we had to dance a waltz and a jive. It was fine and it was soon over.

The winners, of course, were quite rightly Paul and Tim. I reflected that many of us would have been around when people like Paul and Tim would have been put in jail. The judges of the competition, unlike Len, Bruno and Craig, but more like Darcey, had something nice to say about all the competitors. Couple No 9, she said, looked as if they had been waltzing together all their lives. That was me and Heinz.

The band played "Auld Lang Syne" and Gill and I went up to Paul and Tim's suite to open the champagne. When I win a million with my Premium Bonds, and it won't be long now, I shall book a world cruise and a suite. You have not only a sitting room, a study, a circular bath and a balcony, but also your own butler. I know there is the problem of my dogs, Bobby and Joey, but with all that money I am sure something could be arranged.

IN MEMORY OF
GEORGE & OLLIE
GEORGE MELLY
1926-2007
HIS FAULTS DIED WITH HIM
OLLIE
1992-2009
THE CAT WITHOUT FAULTS

CARE AND CONTROL

Chapter 9

If it wasn't for the dogs and dancing, I'd give London a miss in January and February. Ten days after I arrived back from the cruise I got ill, then I heard on the news that the flu jab had only worked for three per cent of the population. I wasn't one of the three per cent and I fell into that category of "vulnerable elderly people for whom flu might cause complications". It did – I got bronchitis on top of it.

I couldn't go to the prison where I work in the visitors' centre every Thursday. I couldn't go to My Memories Café and this time it was something I minded missing very much. Raymond had sweetly offered to come along and dance with any ladies who wanted to. Gill was also coming. One of her six sisters is a beautician and Gill has picked up many of her skills: she was going to do manicures and hand massage. Kate, who organises these afternoon activities, had indicated to Raymond which ladies were likely to want to dance. And he went up to them, made a small bow and said, "Could I have this dance?"

Some people with dementia find that they can still

remember and derive pleasure from poems learnt while at school, or from favourite music, whether Mozart or Bing Crosby, even though more recent memories have faded. Of course, the women loved Raymond asking them to dance so elegantly. It's an activity that will be repeated and next time I'll be there. Perhaps I'll be able to get some of the men up on their feet. I might have more success than I did with George. He had so much rhythm, but it was all expended in his singing. At most he'd hop about on the stage to Dr Jazz but nothing would get him onto the dance floor.

It was because of George having dementia that I had become involved and interested in the subject. I had some understanding of how the person with dementia felt, and I knew from experience how isolated carers can be.

Dementia is notoriously difficult to diagnose in its early stages. And with someone like my husband, who had always been eccentric and absent-minded, it was even harder.

Three years before he died, I just thought his behaviour was becoming somewhat delinquent. He was losing credit cards – fourteen in one month – because he couldn't remember his PIN, which should have been easy as it was related to his birthday. He would leave the front door open, lose his keys, and when travelling to London he would sometimes end up in

Plymouth. I didn't take these episodes seriously. Then something happened which should have alerted me but still didn't. He was singing at Ronnie Scott's, and when I called in the club, admittedly unexpectedly, he didn't recognise me. A few weeks later – this was January 2005 – his lung cancer was confirmed and I think I was putting his increasing memory lapses – which weren't just forgetting the names of his favourite film stars, Laurel and Hardy – down to his health, his whiskey and his medication. George had pills for his heart, high cholesterol, psoriasis, duodenal ulcers and a thyroid problem – also numerous inhalers for his lungs.

But in March that same year I stopped him in the street outside our house, and again he failed to recognise me. When I told him my name he asked if I was a cousin. We laughed it off, but when I told a friend, she said it wasn't funny, and she thought he had dementia. I went to my GP, who gave me the number of admiral nurses; she said they helped anyone worried about any aspect of dementia.

I rang them and got through to Madeline; she listened carefully and said it sounded like vascular dementia with Lewy bodies.

The next few years were often sad and depressing but as it was George there was a lot of humour; also love and anger. Hate too, because sometimes when he was unfair, I hated him and then I hated myself as well.

When his diagnosis was confirmed I felt relief. Not knowing in any situation is hard, but knowledge is power. Madeline sent me information packs, advised which books to buy and told me which financial benefits we were entitled to. I now googled not only lung cancer but vascular dementia, Alzheimer's and Lewy body too. A diagnosis also meant that I wasn't imagining things; there was something wrong and now I could plan.

There were the two conditions to consider – the cancer and the dementia. I planned for stair rails, a wheelchair, a commode. I imagined moving him from his bedroom, which was on the second floor – too many stairs – down to his sittingroom. And eventually all these things came to pass. I hoped he would die of cancer before he reached the last stages of dementia when he might have to go into a home. And there I think we were lucky, because he did die. At least I think we were. It's probably selfish and sentimental, but because I miss him, I sometimes wish he was still in his sitting room, in his hospital bed or even in a home and I was on my way to visit. When you miss someone it's not just the good bits and the happy times; you miss the whole person, the bad bits – and the sad bits too.

I knew that it was important to George to keep working. Singing wasn't a problem; right up to about four weeks before he died he could remember all the words to his songs. Writing was different. When asked to write 1000 words on Salvador Dali he wrote 10,000. It was a frightful muddle, scrawled over endless sheets of paper without numbers, and three months late. Luckily he had a wonderful editor who sorted it out.

After that I tried to answer his phone so that I could turn down any commission that I thought would be too difficult – but of course that had to be balanced with not assuming too much control.

I was always nervous when George was away singing. I was told that once or twice he'd wandered off to the pub and been unable to find his way back to the concert hall. But some of the battles we had when George's dementia was in the early stage were because I tried to control him and he resisted. My faults and virtues are inextricably linked; I'm a good manager and organiser and therefore I'm bossy and some would say domineering.

But in the end I did learn. It's probably wrong to make comparisons between dementia sufferers and teenagers, but a useful strategy when in conflict with either is to walk away. I did it with my own teenagers and then I did it with George. And I learnt to be kinder sometimes when he knew that something couldn't possibly be as he imagined it. His eyes would look sad and scared, and then I could put my arms around him.

Later on, in his last few weeks, we could even make jokes. He would ask, "Is such and such true or is that my dementia?" He got to be rather proud of having it, and it was almost the first thing he told people. "What's that thing I've got that starts with D?" he would say. And then he would laugh because he could never remember what it was called. His way of describing his condition was "I have no sense of time, date or place". And one aspect that he enjoyed was possibly caused by Lewy bodies. Three lovely pre-Raphaelite women used to wander through his room and into his bathroom.

It was in March a year before he died that his condition began to deteriorate, although some things remained quite intact – like his refusal to have any treatment for his lung cancer, and his determination to get through three packets of cigarettes a day.

He also began to lose weight; his famous suits hung off him and he lived in his kaftan. I could chart his decline by the contents of our fridge and freezer and the food he liked: fish fingers replaced fish cakes, shepherd's pie was replaced by one lightly scrambled egg. He could only manage three sips of his daily glass of lager and eventually he didn't even want any whiskey.

In June, four weeks before he died, he was carried downstairs for a family lunch in the garden. He sat there with Tom reading *King Lear*, and choosing the bit he wanted read at his funeral. We couldn't carry him back up so he slept in our granddaughter's room next to his sitting room, where the next day the hospital bed was installed. The commode, a box of controlled drugs and a syringe driver arrived, along with the district nurse, the palliative care nurse and a carer called Mary who was going to relieve me for two hours a day.

I found the task of caring for George that last month very satisfying and comforting. I like taking care of people, and because our marriage had often been difficult, I felt I could make up for some of the bad times. I was lucky; I had wonderful support from the nurses, our GP, my friends and children and of course from Madeline.

George's dietary needs went from a spoonful of rice pudding to sucking water from a sponge. I think it was the absence of whiskey that made him less angry and confrontational. The main thing he insisted on was that people should not ask him how he was. I put a note on the door; "Don't ask him," it said, "he will reply 'I'm fucking dying'". And he wanted to. The last ten days when the Marie Curie nurse arrived at night and I went to bed he said goodbye rather than good-night. And then, four weeks after he had managed to sing three songs at a benefit for admiral nurses, he died. At home, not in pain and ready to go.

———————————

Working at the prison visitors' centre and helping at My Memories Café were not the only things I missed while I was ill: there was also the monthly dances at Shoreditch Town Hall, the Porchester Hall, often on a Friday and just up the road, and Watford, a bit of a trek but worth it. Dino and Dora went to Shoreditch and afterwards came to see me. They sat in front of the fire and told me that Mr Wonderful had sent his love. Seeing that I wasn't well enough to go out for supper, Dino went to my kitchen and produced pasta carbonara without asking me where anything was. Having washed up – he doesn't like dishwashers any more than computers – he inspected my medicines. He told me to take the stronger of the two antibiotics I had been given. No alcohol, he said, lots of yoghurt, Greek honey and keep well lubricated. Dora made my bed look more inviting and when they left I couldn't decide whether I felt three years old or a hundred.

The next day I booked a holiday in Tenerife. As I was sitting in Gatwick Airport, Dino sent me a text: "Turn off the air-con in your hotel, they never clean the filters and you can pick up germs that way."

I'M AN ANGEL

Chapter 10

The first time I described what I thought of as my angel costume to George, he said, "Angel? You were Cupid." The costume I was describing – wings, bow and arrow, G-string and a flimsy bra – was the one I wore when I was working in Murray's Cabaret Club. It was 1953 and I was nearly sixteen. The club employed hostesses and if you could dance at all you could double up as a dancer. My part as an angel in the wedding scene was a small one. I had to flit across the floor, pointing my bow and arrow at the bride and groom, do a few twirls, then stand very still at the back of the stage and whip my bra off while the curtains closed to hide my skinny body from the audience. In those days you could be naked on stage as long as you didn't move and it looked "tasteful".

My other role was as a nurse in the London Town scene. I decided to tell my mother only about this part. My previous job had been working in a grim little shop in Oxford Street, and although she was pleased that I seemed less grumpy and was earning more money, she worried about the nature of the job. But a nurse! I didn't mention the brevity of the dark-blue cape that showed my G-string while I tap-danced across the stage in the London Town scene. And for the first month I didn't tell her that when I wasn't on stage I was sitting with a customer who was being cajoled into buying me cigarettes and flowers. And dancing with them too, if you could call it that; I don't think Raymond or Dino would. The night club shuffle was easier than sitting with a customer and trying to think of something to say.

The cabaret club job had been advertised in *The Stage*: "Good looking girls, 5' 6" minimum height with some dancing experience required in well-established West End night club". I thought my three years learning ballet and acrobatics with Miss Betty Brooks could count as experience. I was quite good at ballet and passed my grades with top marks. My acrobatics were very good. I could do the splits with either left or right leg in front and I could bend over backwards and pick up a handkerchief with my mouth. I could turn cartwheels in a neat circle and walk across a room on my hands. I wish I could still do those things, but no longer do I wish I could run away and join a circus.

We lived in a village with no cinema, but there was a hall owned by the British Legion and every Christmas Miss Betty Brooks put on a show. I expect there were lots of acts but the only one I remember is mine.

Wearing green satin pants and bra and covered with a black net see-through slip, I pranced and high-kicked across the stage while the teenage boys whistled and shouted from the back. The acrobatic skills have helped with yoga, but more importantly, Dino said the ballet would help with the ballroom dancing.

Recently I turned up for a lesson with Dino without my shoes. The traffic had been too bad for me to think of going back for them, and anyway, I'd remembered that Dino had told me to practise barefoot.

"Wonderful, darling, I'll teach you to dance with your feet."

In his studio he taught me how to use the balls of my feet as we practised the rumba. I had to point my feet and he showed me when to use the outside or the inside edge. He explained that in any Latin dance my weight should always be forward. I got lots of "good girl, good girl". Or when it wasn't quite perfect he said, "I'll accept that."

I was looking forward to the next tea dance when I could show off my new skill.

But the tea dance at the Porchester was a failure. Perhaps I can only do the rumba in bare feet.

We went out for a coffee afterwards. "What happened?" said Dino. "No tidy feet, butcher hands and you got all tense." I felt miserable.

It's not that Dino teaches complicated steps or

routines. What he cares about is timing and musicality. But there is a conflict between my brain trying to remember the steps and my soul needing to respond to the music. These days if I wake in the night, ten past three is my usual time, instead of counting backwards from a hundred in sevens I say walk, swivel, change weight. Walk, swivel, change weight.

I think Dino has imagined those few years with Miss Betty Brooks to be something they were not. "Ballerina!" he says. "Posture, stick out your tits, point your feet." I point my feet and thrust my very flat chest forward. Its quite hard doing all that and relaxing at the same time.

Dino is off on business for a week so I am taking advantage of his absence by having a sort of mini-lesson with Dora. This lesson will have many advantages. I won't have that anxious-to-please thing that I seem to have with men, doubly so if they are also my teachers. We have arranged to meet on Saturday in Kensington Gardens, and as long as it doesn't rain I'll have my lesson there. We are meeting my friend Nell who is going to bring sandwiches and hold the dogs, hers and mine.

It's wonderful. Only very small problems: Joey's flexi-lead gets tangled up in my legs as I do the swivel bit, Bobby chases after a large German shepherd and Iris, Nell's dog, tries to steal someone's picnic. I feel quite pleased that I did the swivel correctly even though the grass is wet and the path is gravel. Also some small children seem to find my fan position hilarious. Dora then teaches me the heel turn, something Raymond in eighteen months never managed.

DINO'S HAREM

Chapter 11

There is quite a lot of competition for Dino at a social dance. Besides his girlfriend Dora, there's me, Caterina, another of his pupils, a very glamorous Russian, plus all the other women who have noticed that Dino is the best dancer in the room. We are all in love with him and want to be No 1 in the harem. Watching Dino and Dora dance, we all realise we don't stand a chance – their rumba would make a blue movie.

Dino is very Latin. He optimises care and control. He now controls what I eat and my dogs. Like most of my friends, he would like me to put on at least a kilo in weight. When I have supper with him and Dora, he butters little bits of crusty bread and offers them to me. When I seem to be getting stuck with a larger amount of food than I am used to, he divides what I've left on my plate and almost spoon-feeds me with one half, much like I used to when my children were refusing to eat their greens. "Just one more mouthful," I used to say, and so does Dino. He doesn't go as far as to raise a spoon in the air and move it towards my mouth making chuff-chuff noises.

Bobby and Joey are both fifteen, and rather blind and deaf. As a consequence, Joey, who isn't coping very well with his old age, has become rather clingy. "He won't go with you," I say when Dino takes charge of the lead while we're walking in the park. But like me, Joey knows there's a lot of care with all that control, and when Dino decides Joey is getting tired, he allows himself to be picked up and carried. "He doesn't usually allow other people to do that," I say rather feebly.

Tonight a big party of us including Caterina, Dora, a young woman who calls herself "the dance whore" and me are going to the Savoy for a black-tie dinner dance. I'm hoping not to be spoon-fed.

Evening socials often go on till midnight and can be more expensive. There's a spring buffet run by Mr Wonderful in Kingston's working man's club that costs £15. Another one I often go to is run by Elizabeth Anderson, herself a great dancer. It takes place in the SouthSide Ballroom in Wandsworth and the £18 entry fee includes sandwiches, sticks of carrot and cucumber, delicious cake and prosecco plus a demonstration by professional dancers.

The Royal Opera House's monthly tea dance with their own orchestra costs £11 for two hours and the Waldorf's Sunday afternoon tea dance, also with a live band is £59 for three hours.

Dancing needn't be expensive. If you've been dancing for years, are perfectly content with your ability and don't want lessons, you can just go to tea dances, which, at only four or five pounds with tea and cake, are by far the best value. Most towns now have them, although I hear from Gill that this isn't the case in Wales. It seems that there are just a few small church halls that host sequence dances.

Some lucky women who haven't stopped dancing since they started at the Hammersmith Palais seventy years ago are never short of a partner. The other group who never sit down are the very pretty ones. There's one young woman with two left feet that Raymond nick-named her titty bubbles. She's never off the floor. "Call me old fashioned," he says. Well, he's not very PC either.

If like me you do want lessons, there are two options: group or private. Group lessons are usually about eight or ten pounds. You might get two hours followed by some social dancing, but you will often be dancing with people as hopeless as you are.

Private lessons will cost £40–60 an hour depending on how much the teacher is paying for the hall and what level he or she is at. With these lessons you might learn "the whisk with the promenade chassis"; that "the hockey stick" is nothing to do with hitting a ball. You might even attempt the paso doble in which your partner is a matador and you his cape.

Charging me for lessons presented a problem for Dino. I think because of our dog connection and being the same age as his mother, I am now "family" and therefore not allowed to pay for them. We have solved this in a most enjoyable way. I have my lesson, we meet up with Dora and then I take them out to supper. Dino twitches a bit when I get out my credit card, but that's our arrangement and he has to put up with it. He asserts his authority by checking the bill.

The dinner dance at the Savoy tonight is expensive, £125, but there's going to be live music and lots to eat and drink.

I hadn't been to the Savoy since I worked at the cabaret club. Although I never accepted invitations from customers, for some reason I had given my phone number to a rather fat Belgian called Edouard. It might have been because he wasn't pushy and didn't rub himself up against me on the tiny dance floor. Or because he'd bought me two boxes of du Maurier cigarettes and a spray of orchids. Both my mother and I smoked so the cigarettes were welcome and the flowers provided a good profit for the club.

When he rang the next day I was still asleep; my mother hadn't even brought me my breakfast. I never got in before two and she always woke me at midday with tea and toast in bed. She answered the call and told me that a very nice gentleman had invited me to lunch at the Savoy and that she'd accepted for me. I wasn't as cross with her as I pretended to be – after all, what harm could I come to having lunch in a crowded room? And anyway, I'd never been to a posh hotel and I wanted to.

He met me in the foyer and said we would go to his room first as he had a present for me. This was a bit alarming but I didn't want to make a fuss so up we went. The present was a beautiful tortoiseshell box engraved in silver with a statue of Diana the huntress.

"Now," he said, "you can lie on the bed and I will give you a very special kiss. You are very young and still virgin if I am not mistake? You will still be a virgin." I hadn't a clue what he meant; I just knew I didn't want him to kiss me and I began to cry. Edouard stopped going on about the special kiss, told me to wipe my eyes and took me down to the shiny dining room for lunch. He ordered for me: shrimp cocktail and a fancy chicken dish and did his best to help me relax. I hoped the waiters would think he was my grandfather, but remembering my over-made-up face, my pencil skirt and peep-toe shoes, it was rather unlikely. I had three scoops of ice cream, he then put ten five-pound notes in my bag and got the doorman to call a taxi. I've still got the tortoiseshell box, and I didn't remain "virgin" for long.

The Savoy hadn't changed much but I had. Unable to finish my fillet steak I asked the waiter to put it in a doggy bag for Joey and Bobby. That's not something I would have had the nerve to do 63 years ago.

DRESS CODE PROBLEMS

Chapter 12

There is an evening dance tonight in Essex which, being an Essex woman, I am keen to go to. Also Heinz, my favourite dance host from the cruise, is staying with Gill and she is going to drive him and his girlfriend down.

The problem is that it's on the day I'm working in the prison visitors' centre. Dino and Dora have said they will pick me up but there won't be time to go home and change and I can't decide what dress will be suitable for the dance and the prison. Unlike tea dances where some people come in jeans, most of us like the opportunity to dress up for evening events. When I went dancing with Raymond, realising he was a Grace Kelly fan, I used to wear pale-blue floaty chiffon. Dino is 25 years younger and goes more for the Moulin Rouge look, or maybe Liza Minnelli in *Cabaret*? I have a short, shiny, emerald satin skirt which he likes. Although I don't quite dress to please men, nor do I dress to displease them.

I turn up at the centre in a longish, very full, bright-yellow skirt and cover the sequinned top I wore at Margate with a long jumper. All my colleagues are slightly surprised by the full make-up and my hair which I've carefully ironed with my straighteners; in my haste to get ready I have burnt my neck and have covered up the angry-looking red mark with a plaster.

I am not the only one with a dress code problem. A woman has come to visit her husband; she is showing so much flesh that we don't think she will be allowed in. Her top pushes up her breasts into a shape that would rival Dolly Parton's. Also her shorts are so brief that they show a large amount of midriff and her buttocks are only just contained. Peep-toe platform shoes complete the picture.

At work I am considered to be tactful, and due to my age, as having some authority. Also, compared to fellow workers, I sound posh; my manager once told me I sound like Penelope Keith in *The Good Life*. These dubious attributes mean I am given the task of asking the young woman to find something to cover up some bits of her. It's a problem. She is perfectly willing to cover up but what with? As it's a warm day she has come without a coat and I don't want to lend her my ragged jumper and expose my flimsy top.

Luckily it's a biometrics day. On these days the visitors are required to queue three times. Once to show me or a colleague their IDs, then to have their fingerprints done and finally to cross the courtyard that separates the visitors' centre from the main prison building and have their IDs checked yet again. We are assured that once the biometric system is established, the whole process of getting in to see "loved ones" will be speeded up. Meanwhile, people start queuing at one o'clock and are lucky to get in by three o'clock. Visiting stops at four but if anyone complains they are told that the allotted time is only half an hour, so anything more is a bonus.

The only advantage to this lengthy process is that it gives the compliant half-naked visitor time to go home and do a quick change.

She isn't the only one to take advantage of the wait. Two families have come with insufficient IDs. Like most normal people, they assumed that passports would be enough to prove their identity. They are at most prisons but not the one I'm working in. This one requires proof of address as well. People must bring a bill dated within the last three months, but not a mobile phone bill. Not only do some people have little access to utility bills or bank statements, they are often not told of this requirement. Telling people who might have travelled far and have taken the day off work that they won't be allowed in is a deeply unpleasant job. Assuming that it's up to me to allow the visit, they will plead with me to let them in just this once. I explain that if it was up to me I would happily let them in and usually I apologise for the inefficiency of our system.

It's good news that the two families have bank accounts. They are going to take the bus to the nearest branch of their bank and get them to print them a statement.

It's my lunch break so I'm going to paint my nails and ring Dora to tell her that my manager has said I can go a bit early.

I tell Dora about the naked lady. She is a free spirit and doesn't see why the visitor has to cover herself up. I think many of the rules are stupid but this one is OK. Not all the prisoners are fortunate enough to have a Dolly Parton lookalike visiting them.

Dora also has a dress problem. This year she is competing in "Stars of the Future", an important competition in Brentwood. She is dancing the foxtrot and the waltz and needs a ball gown. They don't come cheap – £1000 new and there's no fairy godmother. If she buys second-hand from eBay she won't be able to try it on. But at the dance tonight she is hoping to meet a designer who said she is willing to let her have one of her seconds.

On the way there Dino gets an urgent message from the organiser. There's no sound from the speakers or the mic. Dino is reluctant to let me drive; he says I ride the clutch. He pulls over and parks on a lay by while he thinks about the problem.

"You're probably using too many extension leads," he tells Myrtle, the organiser.

I had quite forgotten that the dance has been advertised as a "spring theme ball". It doesn't seem to matter; although Myrtle and her equally glamorous sister are dressed as Venus and Flora from the *Primavera*, no one else has bothered.

Thanks to Dino the sound system is working. The music is a version of "I love Paris in the Spring Time" and the hall looks beautiful. There are tulips on every table and we are given the best one. Myrtle has made a knock-out drink – Sparkling Spring Punch. Heinz wants to know what's in it. Prosecco, Maraschino liqueur and tangerine juice, she tells us. We were all quite jolly anyway. As he's the driver, Dino isn't drinking but he's happy, having gathered some new additions to his harem, some of whom aren't wearing enough to be allowed in to visit a "loved one" in a prison. Gill isn't drinking either she never does but she is proudly showing us some photographs of her new grandchild. Dora has made contact with the woman who will let her have a fabulous ball gown very cheaply. And me? Apparently my posture has improved. Also the punch is delicious.

WHY WE DANCE

Chapter 13

Words and music and dancing – I think the last two are the most evocative and perhaps the oldest forms of expression.

Ancient man and woman danced, just as some birds do; not just swans and birds of paradise – many parrots do too. The dung beetle dances to orientate himself. Once he's got the dung into a ball he rolls it away from the dung pile in a straight path. This guarantees he won't be competing with the other beetles around the pile. Before rolling his ball he climbs on top of it and dances.

The male peacock spider, whose beautiful rainbow-coloured body outshines not only the peacock but also the costumes of the Latin dancers I saw competing at Blackpool, dances, sings and vibrates to attract the female. If he isn't any good, she eats him.

Apart from Asian elephants, who dance to Bach played on the violin (see remarkable YouTube video), I can't think of any other animals that do. I don't count dogs who are trained to dance with treats or bears who are tortured to do so. The dung beetle dances to protect his food; the spider and the birds dance to attract a mate, while humans dance for a variety of reasons.

To take his mind off his troubles a friend from Shoreditch has become obsessed with the Argentine tango. His daughter is bipolar and refuses to speak to him. From the little I know of him it's hard to understand why. We often talk about it when Mr Wonderful is playing anything other than the Argentine as that is the only dance he gets up for. He seems to me to be kind and clever and I can see how hurt he is by the breakdown of this relationship. How can you mend something if there isn't any communication? All he can do is forget about it for a few hours a week while he is dancing. And Gill, when her marriage started to unravel, she took up ballroom. "When I'm dancing," she said, "nothing else seems to matter except the music; it seems to put the life back in me." The husband of a young woman who helps me with the heavy work in the garden went to prison last year and she started to learn the salsa. "I didn't want another man," she said. "It just stops me feeling so lonely."

It helps me too; when my daughter Candy was diagnosed with second-stage terminal cancer I found that dancing could occasionally make me think about something else. When my son died of a heroin overdose in 1980 I drank, I got stoned and I spent a month in a psychiatric hospital. When George died aged 80 of lung cancer and vascular dementia, his doctor said, "That was the best death I've ever seen." She meant he looked peaceful, he was home in his own bed and the dementia wasn't too advanced.

His attitude to his death, and he knew he was dying, is an example I hope I will be able to follow. I can't think of anything else he set a good example for – well, not in the conventional sense.

The letters, the tributes and the arrangements helped with the sad period that followed. Much as I endlessly complained about him, we had been together for nearly 50 years.

Candy received her diagnosis in late 2007, the same year that George died. All her family were excited about the baby she was expecting, but were devastated by the completely unexpected diagnosis she received three days after Nancy was born. She was sitting up in bed nursing the baby when two doctors came in and sat on the bed. Always a bad sign. The older one said, "We've got the result of the biopsy. The tumour in your back is secondary breast cancer." Her husband Mark was there when I left and I sat on the 148 bus doing what comes naturally to me – I rang all my friends. I also left a message with my doctor. She rang me back the next day and when I asked her what it meant she said, "Her life will be considerably shortened."

"How long"?

"She might have five years."

She did, she had five years, nine months and two weeks .

Montaigne wrote about a king who when captured saw his neighbour being led away to prison, then his son led away to his death. The king only wept when he saw what happened to his neighbour. When questioned about it he replied, "One event can be marked with tears, the other is beyond expression."

Sometimes Candy went into remission, sometimes it seemed as if the drugs and the chemo could win. She came to Spain with me when Nancy was just one and she went to Goa with Mark and Nancy three years later. They moved out of London to live on the south coast and as usual she made many new friends.

She'd asked me to be her chemo friend, and once I went with her to the hospital and we sat there with the chemo trickling through her. I caught a train back and arrived in time to go to a tea dance in the Camden Centre near King's Cross. Sometimes when she went into the hospice for a rest, I took the dogs and stayed at a dog-friendly hotel and then went to be with her. When she closed her eyes and I got up to leave, she would say, "Don't go. No need to talk, just sit and knit like you used to." When she was well enough we would go for rather slow walks in her local park. The metal vertebrae in her back made it ache and she often had to rest on a bench.

Unlike George, she battled with the cancer and almost until the end she thought she could win. When she knew she couldn't, like George she planned her funeral, a big party in a place overlooking the sea.

Three months before she died, we were warned that the steroids that were keeping her alive would suddenly stop working; they did and she died, aged 52, at home surrounded by all her family.

In the ten days between her death and her funeral I went to Majorca, where Mr Wonderful had organised a dance holiday.

I'd been grieving for Candy since my doctor had said five years; I was still grieving but I went. The space needed to be filled with something. Anything.

Acknowledgements

Thank you Susannah for landing me a contract at Short Books; Joan for kick-starting the project by sending a chapter to the *Oldie*; Christina for walking Bobby and Joey, and Sylvia for cleaning my house so I could go dancing; Dora for a new friendship; Malcolm (Mr Wonderful) for the best music to dance to; Andrée, Nell, Jane and Anula for patiently reading early drafts; Penelope for chapter 13; Carmen whose encouragement I can't write without; and Aurea, Klara and Rebecca who have turned my words into a proper book.

Praise for *Take a Girl Like Me* by Diana Melly:
(Chatto & Windus, 2005)

Hardly short of a masterpiece, this book brilliantly evokes
the frenetic egotism of Bohemian life of the sixties.
– Hugh Massingbird, *The Daily Telegraph*

Told with panache...its pages fizz with gaiety.
– *Mail on Sunday*, Book of the Week

This well-written memoir is wonderful because it
is so naturally contrary to the notion that a memoir
should paint over everything and make the author
shine... She makes her life quite present to the reader
– even those parts where she wasn't particularly present
herself – and that is the sort of gift to posterity
that posterity can remember.
– Andrew O'Hagan, *Sunday Times*

It is rare to find a book that describes a marriage with
such breathtaking intimacy as Diana Melly does
in her autobiography, *Take a Girl Like Me*. She writes
the story of her grippingly unconventonal life with
an astonishing yet matter-of-fact frankness.
– Nicholas Haslam, *The Spectator*

Hers is an extraordinary story, exceptionally well told.
– *Independent on Sunday*